NEW MO JOURNAL

Record your special journey using words and pictures and create a family keepsake to treasure forever.

MW00876305

Mom Name

_____

Baby Name

_____

Date of Birth

_____

Date:_____

Date:_____

_____
_____
_____

Date:_____

_____

_____

_____

Date:_____

_____

_____

_____

Date:_____

Date:_____

_____

_____

_____

Date:_____

_____

_____

_____

Date:_____

_____
_____
_____

Date:_____

_____
_____
_____

Date:_____

_____

_____

_____

Date:_____

_____
_____
_____

Date:_____

_____

_____

_____

Date:_____

_____

_____

_____

Date:_____

_____
_____
_____

Date:_____

_____
_____
_____

Date:_____

_____

_____

_____

Date:_____

_____
_____
_____

Date:_____

_____

_____

_____

Date:_____

_____

_____

_____

Date:_____

_____

_____

_____

Date:_____

_____

_____

_____

Date:_____

_____

_____

_____

Date:_____

_____

_____

_____

Date:_____

_____

_____

_____

Date:_____

_____

_____

_____

Date:_____

_____

_____

_____

Date:_____

_____

_____

_____

Date:_____

_____

_____

_____

Date:_____

_____
_____
_____

Date:_____

_____
_____
_____

Date:_____

_____

_____

_____

Date:_____

_____

_____

_____

Date:_____

_____

_____

_____

Date:_____

_____

_____

_____

Date:_____

_____

_____

_____

Date:_____

_____

_____

_____

Date:_____

_____
_____
_____

Date:_____

_____

_____

_____

Date:_____

Date:_____

_____

_____

_____

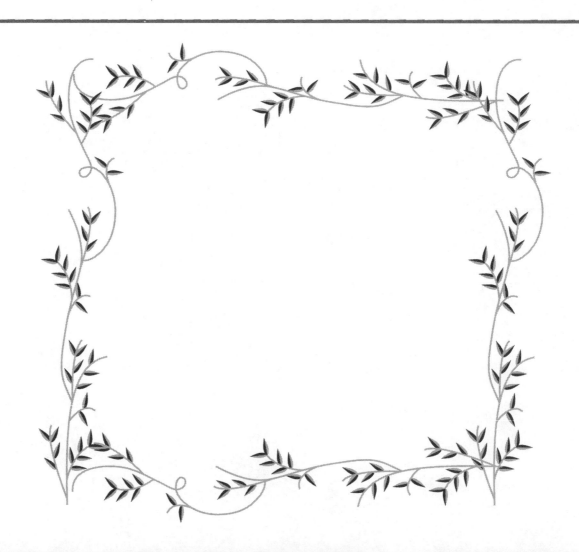

Date:_____

_____

_____

_____

Date:_____

_____

_____

_____

Date:_____

_____
_____
_____

Date:_____

_____

_____

_____

Date:_____

_____

_____

_____

Date:_____

_____

_____

_____

Date:_____

_____

_____

_____

Date:_____

_____

_____

_____

Date:_____

_____

_____

_____

Date:_____

_____

_____

_____

Date:_____

_____

_____

_____

Date:_____

_____

_____

_____

Date:_____

_____
_____
_____

Date:_____

_____
_____
_____

Date:_____

_____

_____

_____

Date:_____

_____

_____

_____

Date:_____

_____

_____

_____

Date:_____

_____

_____

_____

Date:_____

_____

_____

_____

Date:_____

_____

_____

_____

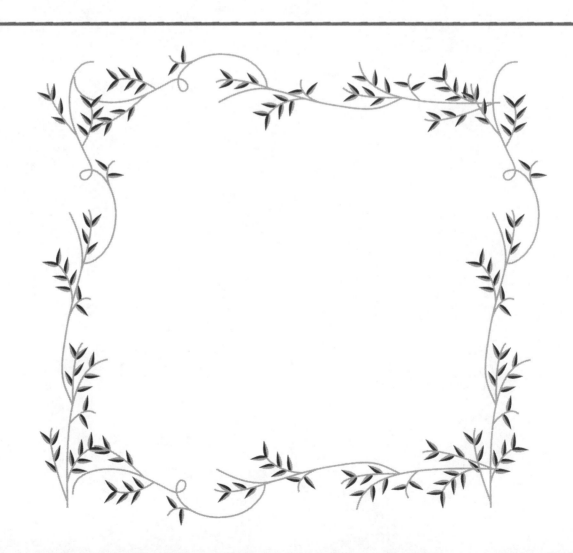

Date:_____

_____

_____

_____

Date:_____

_____

_____

_____

Date:_____

_____
_____
_____

Date:_____

_____

_____

_____

Date:_____

_____

_____

_____

Date:_____

_____

_____

_____

Date:_____

_____

_____

_____

Date:_____

_____

_____

_____

Date:_____

_____
_____
_____

Date:_____

_____

_____

_____

Date:_____

_____

_____

_____

Date:_____

_____

_____

_____

Date:_____

_____

_____

_____

Date:_____

_____

_____

_____

Date:_____

_____

_____

_____

Date:_____

_____

_____

_____

Date:_____

_____

_____

_____

Date:_____

_____

_____

_____

Date:_____

_____

_____

_____

Date:_____

_____

_____

_____

Date:_____

Date:_____

_____

_____

_____

Date:_____

_____

_____

_____

Date:_____

_____

_____

_____

Date:_____

_____
_____
_____

Date:_____

_____

_____

_____

Date:_____

_____

_____

_____

Date:_____

_____
_____
_____

Date:_____

_____

_____

_____

Date:_____

_____
_____
_____

Date:_____

_____

_____

_____

Date:_____

_____

_____

_____

Date:_____

_____

_____

_____

Date:_____

_____

_____

_____

Date:_____

_____

_____

_____

Date:_____

_____

_____

_____

Date:_____

_____

_____

_____

Date:_____

_____

_____

_____

Date:_____

_____

_____

_____

Date:_____

_____

_____

_____

Date:_____

_____

_____

_____

Date:_____

_____

_____

_____

Date:_____

_____

_____

_____

Date:_____

_____

_____

_____

Date:_____

_____

_____

_____

Date:_____

_____

_____

_____

Date:_____

_____

_____

_____

Date:_____

_____

_____

_____

Date:_____

_____

_____

_____

Date:_____

_____
_____
_____

Date:_____

_____
_____
_____

Date:_____

_____

_____

_____

Date:_____

_____

_____

_____

Date:_____

_____

_____

_____

Date:_____

_____

_____

_____

Date:_____

_____

_____

_____

Date:_____

_____

_____

_____

Date:_____

_____

_____

_____

Made in the USA
San Bernardino, CA
22 June 2020

74026848R00076